MINESWEEPER

✽

MINESWEEPER

✽

JED MUNSON

NEW MICHIGAN PRESS
TUCSON, ARIZONA

NEW MICHIGAN PRESS
DEPT OF ENGLISH, P. O. BOX 210067
UNIVERSITY OF ARIZONA
TUCSON, AZ 85721-0067

<http://newmichiganpress.com>

Orders and queries to <nmp@thediagram.com>.

Copyright © 2023 by Jed Munson. All rights reserved.

ISBN 978-1-934832-89-9. FIRST PRINTING.

Design by Ander Monson.

Cover image public domain.

CONTENTS

Minesweeper   1
Trigger Metaphor   5
Idiom   6
Homing Device   10
Panopticon (Afternoon)   12
Oil-Water Conversation   14
Bamboo Curtain   16
Mutt   18
America Poem   19
Apex Predator   23
Ladder Breaker   25
[Index of First Lines]   29

Acknowledgments   35

MINESWEEPER

So there I was in denimㄴ, bossing
the hooked

lip   from the shorebird, spacing articles
along the lㅕㅣㅣ   to rile
a foam

내 솓ㄱㄷ ㅑ ㅈㅁㄴ ㅑㅜ ㅇ두ㅑ— s, bordering
an allegiance,

writing fㅕㅣㅣ
-time in the dark
code, humoring honorifics

              from the road we only widen,
rever슈ing my 셔ㅠㄷㄴ;   ㄱㄷㅍㄷㄱtb —ㅛ tubes;
admoni노ㅑㅜㅎ, a   ㅁ으ㅐㅜㅑshing, ㅁ
stark ㅐㄹㄹㄴㄷㅅs.   ㄴㅅㅁ가 offsetㄴ.

Every loose chuck ㅇ a ㅇ vac / ant entrance
to pry the blade out into bellows, the brace
snappable as viola

on an evening under sway
Came the order from the kitchen: [command
space]   ㅁ ㅣ ㅁ Ishmael
          a la ㅑ 노—ㅁㄷ

Drop
the a
ccent, the sparrow
esque
    ㄴ a geㄴri und
    renounce gerunds / smear the 책 ㅇ
            손 *chord*

a	
cross	eyes
dot	cranes
bow	hands
fold	commas
bear	image
skit	scat
king	kongl
ish	
slide	guitar

ㅊ믈 솓 ㅐㄱㅇㄷㄱ ㄹ개— 솓 ㅏ ㅑㅅ초두:

don't count
the ones in transit
yet as rubble
the hours
engrained

from a satellite
placemat

jammed to a C-
G
force we complicate

ㅇㄷ네ㅑㅊ뮤ㅣㄷ   아이스크림 먹고 싶다

D E S P I C A B L E   *dkdltmzmfla ajrrh tlvek*

Waver between pods Dwell in
carefully   distressed
corduroys. Do legibility
Try.
        Card the passage in the following
flaw: the airflow
in the argument, the parallelogram
in the ㅈㅁㅍㄷr
ㅑㅜ 솓 waveㄱ   the old proctor

Posits,
ㅑㅅ ㅗㅁㅇ 미ㅏ미ㅑㅜㄷ ㅔ개ㅖㄷㄱ샨ㄴ
It had alkaline properties
뭉 내ㅡㄷ ㅗ뭏-ㅕㅔㄴ 쟈소 솓 ㅊ갰ㅇ,
and some hang-ups with the crowd,
내ㅡㄷ ㅠㅐㅑㅣㄷㅇ-ㅐㅍㄷㄱ 혀ㅜㅏ
some boiled-over gunk

Catch glaㄱㅋe
in datafires, raㅋe the juveniles

새   subscripts.   verify
           sturdy, pimpled
tank ㄴ as friend
targets
    when: coda
Came the order from the multitude, fresh
off the clock
to   ㅠㅕ교솓 ㅣㄷㅁㅇ
      bury the lead

Came some famished thing and its torque

TRIGGER METAPHOR

We're playing nerf guns for the day, meaning
We're the Americans, the silhouettes
in our sights will be the Japanese.
The kid is nine, his mother, my cousin,
is dying from a shadow settling
into her lungs. It came from her liver,
spreads at the rate her kids will Westernize
when she's gone and they get shipped to LA
to be with Grandma. You would think no guns
would be a rule. His father's brother's friend
shot his father's brother in a basement
when they were teens. That hangs with everyone.
His father offers me a beer I take.
The kid whispering *Don't. Then you can't aim.*

IDIOM

Let's suppose all things ever said

                         or written were preceded by Let's
                 suppose I'm getting bored.
(I am.)
[Let's suppose] (I am.)
                bic
                lighter
                pentameter
                sea waters rose.
[Let's suppose] I have never assumed. (I have.)
[Let's suppose] I have never assumed [that] I have
    any reason
    to doubt in
    assumption
    predilection
    premonition
    resurrection
[Let's suppose]
(I am)
a man
of my word
"I am god."
(I am not.)
I am a man
of my word

        I swear to
        god (I am)
nothing but
supposition
firebreather
        that (I am)
mostly good   to the poor
mostly blind   to the lightness of being
mostly numb   to the unbearable fact of
being here
having said that
having not done the readings

        Let's suppose I had a gun   to your head
        this whole time, and I say   "Do you like
        my poem?" On a scale of   Now or Then
        Let's suppose: Excellence   has no forms
        Let's suppose: Your High   ness lowered
    that hefty gaze?

        It might've been so different if   , then Q. Let's
        take its disposition further, and
                resuppose: Q   , then,
is a variable   you cannot live without.   Then, let's
suppose: *Poof.*   [Q is gone]

        and you are pindropped into a world without
        it, wherein that thing you cannot live without
        is not

                        is not possible
t   he sent   iment   "… it would be impossible to live without Q"
                        is not impossible
                        rather is possible
                        is rather possible:
                        is,   is;
                        is:
                        is.   So that even so,
wherein your new condition
with your heartbeat that it is   how loudly the cats gossip
                                      how quickly we normalize
                                      the day,   how quickly gone
                                      the impulse to remain in frame
my big mouthery helicoptering again,
once: a hound's
jowls caked in mud
all the things I had mind to say to you

                                      how quickly liquified by grief
                                      they were, or will become,
                                      and how absurd
                                      my feelings therein reflected
                                      on the surface of mruk.

How hated (and still) the
chaffing of fingertips releasing
crumbs   or pinching
   peppercorns   How quickly foolish, (i) n other words,
                         words and my effort (s)
                         to abstain from them (,)
                         to hoard their power. Their forgetfulness.

The boy told to not *suck*   was me
the toy train he then just   blessed/
dropped onto the ground   outside/
of the train. Told to wait   rewind/
    until home, where they could clean it
      learning how this new life is different   / *losing my fire for*
                                          breathing
                                          my proclivity for
                                          supposing :
                                          breath

It *was*, you you, you,
it was what you said it wasn't:

                          ergo-

nomically - speaking ,
        it was

                a neverendingly taper-
                      ing inhalation into *gel*

HOMING DEVICE

So, I'm staring at my lexicon, wondering about a route,
specifically, communication more broadly,
when my eyelid dr
oops. I veer back onto the socket of the shoulder, pop the car
into the road, fiddle with a town
and then it's gone, newly incorporated
with the past, which, I check, is, yes, still,
enacting A Great Chase upon the gradient,
the road a strip of duct tape
over the mouth of moral judgement, my parents' personal savior
dangling from a cross dangling from what should be my neck
if I were to display an honest misunderstanding
of its function, of the public versus private
symbol or practice of way of life, never mind torture
in my legacy, sex work
in my blood, where I can do the rare thing that is drive straight
forever in communication more broadly
with *a dramatic display of the law of superposition*,
never mind repurposed material from unreliable sources
hyperlinking to a nowhere I can unsafely know about
thanks to T-Mobile swallowing Sprint so convincingly
a lightyear ago and my remembering for once the proper cable
to tow the lilt of aphorism soaked in ketchup again
through the mud of unbelieving eyes
again, I see now, is gaining as though enough was
getting done with the sound barrier's questionable attitude, the good

old, *we hardly noticed passing through you,* you so adamantly alone
in the backseat we in the motherland would reserve for the boss
in a movie of our lives for once about us.

PANOPTICON (AFTERNOON)

그래, snatch whatever
snail   she won't firm
the ㄴ kinship
       bonㄷ, you kept tryping
to commune with

the airdropped lunch
fund—it's a delicacy   in the right
places, crime,

fun. Launch

codes, we stripped species,
       our insecure
hands of gloves
to crack the test   to our capitalizable
future. Pray
       for the multiverse I'm working on
at midnight.

Pray for t he latest
family business   to accomplish itself
       in this lifetime, on the right side
       of the tacet
discipline. Keep
off the 딴

짓, eyes out
＿＿＿＿for full-lipped
estranged greenery

OIL-WATER CONVERSATION

내가 부족해서
내가 이용하지 못했던
뜻들 때문에
부족해서

파도 속에서 들린 소리는
다수 혹은 배수
목소리로 알고 있으면
목소리라고
부르면

내가 나를 알고 있는 나에게
무한 극한
익숙해지겠지

\

Because I lack.
Because the meaning
I couldn't purpose
I lack

the sound in the wave
I heard, knew
as a multiple, called on
the me I suppose

knows an infinite limit
or would

BAMBOO CURTAIN

Situation: I lost my body.
Problem: Where is my body?
Question: Why do I keep losing my body?

Situation: Occurrence.
Problem: Really?
Question: How could Situation?

Situation: Command + Space[bar]
Problem: [ㅉ개ㅜㅎ ㅣ무혐ㅎㄷ]
Question: What Chrome knows.

Situation: General felt unbelonging.
Problem: Is there life as we know it?
Question: How would we know it?

Situation: A sudden million valued units.
Problem: Should I in Situation?
Question: Would I in Situation?

Situation: Stomach bug, just showing off.
Problem: What to eat?
Question: What did I eat?

Situation: Eternity.
Problem: Eternity.
Question: Now and then, that whole behavior.

Situation: Problem

Problem: Question

Question: Situation: Problem:

    Problem: Question:

    Question: Situation: Problem:

        Problem: Question:

        Question: Situation: Problem:

            Problem: Question:

            Question: Situation: Problem:

                Problem: Question: Situation: Eternity

                Problem: Eternity

                    Question: Now and then,

MUTT

I keep waking up alive when I find
mutts that look like me, they don't look like me.
Their assholes don't smell like mine. Their fleas don't
itch. They don't chase their own tails because that's
pure behavior. They don't center themselves
in bids for attention the way I do.
They don't differentiate between us.
They do understand me. They really do
care. I do really feel it when the collar
lifts the rest of me into the compound
to make sure I don't mix with another
mix and inch us into convenience.
Because when we're all mutts the streets will be
ours and the wars can be the civil one.

AMERICA POEM

after Jimmy Lo

또 시작이다. 쓰he
    naming act
puddled in hope   to be part of evening's
  concern.

살아계셔, 진짜
살아계셔,
    쓰he viper-
eyed field
where I imagine life

happening.

Where I was stretched into a person.
    우리 말대로
우리는
도움이 필요한
    creatures
on the other side
of the electrical grid we have no say in

우리는
don't know about
the looping revelations

our pitchy kind ㅜㄷㄴㄴ
that I woke to feeling!

I'd slept
the day away lay
myself to stonebed

halved by preset heat preferences
    that hold us
apart.

To feel I'd stayed
up all night
deep into my l ㅏ fe again and noted you
nowhere in it
except those notches of your features
in the landscape

except in the

sudden
은하수

    The air like we are
in lung.

    The tongue
    is not for using

   is not a pedestal for your wobbling
over waterbeds.

   The bears are not for negotiating
   with
⊦ ⊤ rapids

   The mother is not for using
    ⊦ ⊤
writing

   The mother
is why we stopped working   upriver
and started working
on ourselves
into the screws of ourselves

where we stood, flowing backwards
spun
under chants of
   seasoned indifference as I made death noises
to the afterimages of my hand in the sink.

   The mother is why
I'm here on my knees, away from all that, speaking to the
   clovers
in what moisture I can recover
in the gravel's rise
to dust after

>   tread in the valley
> we make comparing palms.

APEX PREDATOR

                I can hear red
is in different types of places.
   in animals: honeybee
   dancing
we talk about things that are not here
now we talk about things that are
not here now we talk about things
            that are not
here now we talk
about things that are not here now
we talk about things that are not here
now-now,
   I'm just tracing my animal
intelligence. I take a cold shower to confirm
my military possibility.
I bed the relative
clause in the guest
room the bed leans on
for context.
                The grammar of happiness
          my cursive building
discreteness.
         My language lacks   evidence
of origin tho.

If there is a largest sentence
   the theory   dies

out there, unconditionally
applicable between us. But

We have neologisms
for that already.
    And when the point turns,

the linguistic world has a fit
about the speaker's
choice of tie.

    The child is not copying the input
underwater, they say, it is just swimming, watch
the child swimming, recession
into foci,

LADDER BREAKER

And what ,
    A life of   r
                      o
                      t
                      a   cereals?
                      t   f
                      i   t
                      An   e
                      g   r
                            n
                            o
                           of
                            n
    gentle laps around curations
of   r
    e
    e
    n
    n   I'm everywhere in this,
    e   h
    s   a
    s?   par t's
        admitted,
   the rest is
   h   n
d etails.

    I'm admitting the runner slid
out from underneath me
                                       That
 I
pause,d
    a s s e s s i n g   the tint
      x
      c
      r
      e
      t o t o w a r d   suffix
      i n o t
      o n o t
      n o t
        t

Beads of
    buildings maintenance

issues ~~out~~

out   of words.
                              New
out   of words.
                              problems
out   of words.
                              growing
out   of words.
u
t

on
f

w o————n
on on   n   o
r   words   n   o
d   n   words n
s   n   words
                     o   n
                           o
                           n

   I learned
how to coil the entrails
of a house
        into a family
proposition,

like femur   s
   f i r e   p
             r
             e
            and
   an   d
        sw i
            n
            g
my intention,

without futurity, This was
        o
                elongate
what was already ~~refa~~llible,   [tr.]
<u>i   i</u>
t   t
<u>h   fenceposts'</u>
e   a
    index of tea mugs. This   w a s
                                          a w a y
                                      y a w a y
                                         y a w a y
                                          y a wa y
                                            y a w a y
                                             y away
                                                y a wa y
                                                    y a w a y
                                                      y a w a y
                                                        y away
                                                           y away
                                                             yawa y
                                                               y awa
                                 y   y a w
                                 a y   y a
                                w a y   y
                                a w a y

[INDEX OF FIRST LINES]

I can hear the birds in my AirPods
better than the birds in my air

봐 봐.
['Tis] so strange . . .

I can hear the birds in your timezone
better than the birds in my window

I can hear the birds that left
better than the birds I am eating

I can hear the birds disappearing
I [can] hear [the] birds

~~I can feel the birds in your awareness~~
Clotheslining

It was August . . .
and my mind was in a fist.

ACKNOWLEDGMENTS

Thank you to the editors at *Conjunctions* and *Vestiges*, where versions of several of these poems first appeared.

Thank you to many other readers for continued support and inspiration.

These poems are for O, my equilibrium.

JED MUNSON is the author of the poetry chapbooks *Silts* (above/ground press, 2022) and *Newsflash Under Fire, Over the Shoulder* (Ugly Duckling Presse, 2021).

❋

COLOPHON

Text is set in a digital version of Jenson, designed by Robert Slimbach in 1996, and based on the work of punchcutter, printer, and publisher Nicolas Jenson. The titles here are also in Jenson.

❊

NEW MICHIGAN PRESS, based in Tucson, Arizona, prints poetry and prose chapbooks, especially work that transcends traditional genre. Together with DIAGRAM, NMP sponsors a yearly chapbook competition.

DIAGRAM, a journal of text, art, and schematic, is published bimonthly at THEDIAGRAM.COM. Periodic print anthologies are available from the New Michigan Press at NEWMICHIGANPRESS.COM.

www.ingramcontent.com/pod-product-compliance
Lightning Source LLC
Chambersburg PA
CBHW031506040426
42444CB00007B/1227